Road To
HEALING

ANGELA MULVEY

WESTBOW
PRESS®
A DIVISION OF THOMAS NELSON
& ZONDERVAN

WestBow Press books may be ordered through booksellers or by contacting:

WestBow Press
A Division of Thomas Nelson & Zondervan
1663 Liberty Drive
Bloomington, IN 47403
www.westbowpress.com
844-714-3454

Scripture taken from the King James Version of the Bible.

ISBN: 978-1-6642-3825-1 (sc)
ISBN: 978-1-6642-3826-8 (e)

Library of Congress Control Number: 2021912804

Print information available on the last page.

WestBow Press rev. date: 07/12/2021

DEDICATION

This book is dedicated to my husband, Brian. Thank you for all of your support and encouragement. For loving me in my darkest times and never giving up on me or us. To my four boys: Alex, Sean, Matthew, and Austin. You boys have cheered me on and encouraged me. To my mother-in-law, Barbara, thank you for all your support and encouragement. To all the people who have supported me, encouraged me, and prayed for me. You know who you are. Most importantly, God. Without Him I wouldn't be able to write this book.

Heavenly Father, I pray for the person reading Your story. You know what it is they are dealing with. I pray that you give them strength. Let them know they are not alone. Place them in the right places with the right people. I pray that whoever reads this book finds their voice. They find the courage to speak up. I know how hard it is having this control your life. I understand the pain they must be feeling. Father I pray that you speak to them through your story on how you changed my life. In Jesus name I pray. Amen.

CONTENTS

ONE

> "But as for you, ye thought evil against me;
> but God meant it unto good."
>
> GENESIS 50:20

I am writing this book to tell my story on how being sexually abused has affected me. How holding on and not speaking up has caused me a lot of pain. My abuse happened at an early age. I kept It away from everyone, suffering in silence and isolation. I pushed it down and tried to pretend that it never happened. I hated myself. I didn't think there would ever be a way out for me. It consumed my life... every second of every day. It was all I could think about, no matter how many years had passed. It was still with me. I'm writing this book to tell how through Jesus, I was able to overcome. I pray that this book really touches the hearts of those who read it. I pray that whoever reads this book will find Jesus and get the strength they need to speak up, that a story, my story will be able to bring more awareness to sexual abuse for children and even adults. It happens too often, and it needs to stop. We need to be aware of what is going on around us. Be the voice of those who can't use theirs. Be there for them. Let them know they are not alone.

This is my story on how I found healing. I pray it helps at least on person find their healing, too. In the Bible there is a scripture that says "*A thief comes to steal and kill and destroy. I have come so that they may have life and have it in abundance*" (John10:10). Satan didn't and still doesn't want me to live an abundant life. He was doing everything he could to keep me from finding freedom. He wasn't going to let me go.

I was told at a young age that I was called by God to be a minister. God even gave me my name! See, I am the youngest of five kids and the only girl. My mom had four boys. A girl was something she had always wanted. When she was pregnant, she had a girl's name picked out: Kelly Sue. But God told her to name me Angela Dawn because I was going to be the angel of the dawn of their new birth. It was after I was born that my parents started to follow the calling that God had on their lives. My parents are now pastors at a church where they live. All of my life I was in and out of church per usual for a pastor's kid, every time the doors were open, I was there.

Growing up in church, hearing about God, plus the lies that satan was telling me, on top of the sexual abuse I was suffering, I became very confused. I was having a hard time believing what my mom told me, that I was a gift from God. How could that be true? Why would God pick me? Why would He allow this to happen to me? He didn't love me or care for me.

On the outside you would think I was just a happy normal kid. Going to church with my family. Smiling. Little did anyone know on the inside I was screaming. A part of me always wanted to tell. Another part, a bigger part, told me to not say anything. It said no one would believe me, that they would blame me. So, I pushed it down. I tried to ignore the images that would replay over and over in my mind. I was scared to go to sleep. The abuse happened over the course of five years. As I said before I felt trapped in constant fear. The images would replay over and over in my mind. It wasn't just the images, the sounds and the smells as well. It always felt as if it was happening all over again. There was no escape, except for school. School was a safe place for me because I felt like no one could hurt me there. But unfortunately, that safe place was short lived when my mom decided to take me out of school my third-grade year. To this day I still don't know why she took me out of school. The physical abuse finally stopped at the age of ten, but emotionally I was damaged beyond repair. I relived it every day. I couldn't escape it. I thought that if I told someone what was going on in my mind, they would think bad things about me. There was a time when my mom was giving me a bath and she asked if anyone touched me, and I said no. I was terrified to tell her the truth. What would she think? Would she still love me?

I now know that those are lies that satan wanted me to believe. He didn't want me to talk about what happened to me. He wanted me to stay silent. He didn't want me to move past it. The hurt, the images, was keeping me in bondage. Satan's bonadage. Since I was young when it happened, I couldn't fully grasp what was going on. I just knew it didn't seem right. It wasn't just the sexual abuse; it was also how other men talked to me. I was a little girl, I had people older than me telling me what they wanted to do to me. How if I looked a certain way, I would be more beautiful. I started to not like what I saw in the mirror. I didn't think I was pretty. I begin to hate myself. Not knowing how to cope with what I was dealing with, I turned to food. I hid most of the food. I didn't want anyone to know what I was doing. I thought if I was fat no one would bother me. But that didn't happen. What I thought protected me from sexual abuse, put me subject to a whole other kind of abuse: bullying. With every joke and tease, a little part of me died inside. My childhood withered away.

As I got older, I got good at pretending things were good. Smiling was something I was getting good at. No matter how hard I tried not to think about the abuse it was always there. When I was a teenager, I was sexually abused again. Just like before, I didn't tell anyone. I tried to forget about it. But I couldn't. I felt disgusting. I hated myself even more. I started to hate God. I blamed Him for things that were done to me. I didn't want to go to church or have anything to do with Him. I also hated the ones who abused me. That hate grew every day. It became the only thing I was able to feel. That hate controlled my life. Not only did I hate my abusers and God, but I hated myself. I can't tell you how many times I blamed myself. "If I had only done this better, or wore different clothes. Why couldn't I just say something the first time it happened? It's my fault that the abuse keeps happening. I only have myself to blame." I was always picking out things that were wrong with me. I was fourteen. Thinking about these things shouldn't have been what went through my mind. I should have been enjoying my teenage years. Instead, I was losing more of who I was. It was becoming all too much for me to deal with. I didn't want to live.

Throughout all of this, I was still going to church with my parents. I still heard about God and His love. I stopped thinking it was for me. I couldn't pull away from wondering how God could let this happen to me, not once but many times. I got to the point where I thought it was all I would experience in my life. Having a third-grade education kept me back from doing a lot of things. It kept me from trying to make friends. I spent a lot of my time reading books. Not only did it help me learn things, but it was an escape for me. It got me out of my reality. When I read books, I was able to pretend that my life wasn't a mess. I was able to be somewhere other than my life. I had dreams of becoming a writer, I had a love for reading and writing. I just didn't think with my background I would be able to follow my dreams. Not only did I go through sexual abuse, but I didn't have a strong education. I was a nobody. I felt useless and dumb. Damaged. From the time I was thirteen up until I was eighteen, I had a lot of mixed feelings about guys. Part of me wanted the attention that they gave me. Another part didn't want any part of it. I was very confused. I allowed the guys I dated do things to me that I am not proud of. I felt so ashamed. But I was using them to help with the pain I felt. I just didn't know at the time that was what I was doing. I hid a lot of things from my parents. I didn't want them to be disappointed in me. I tried to act like things were good. Things got bad for me when I turned sixteen. I started to hang out with people that weren't the best influence on me. I was able to avoid doing the things everyone else was doing for a time, but I was always curious. They seemed to be having a good time. No worries. Maybe it would help me be able to escape the way I was feeling.

Chapter

TWO

---

*"For I know the thoughts that I think toward
you, saith the LORD, thoughts of peace, and
not of evil, to give you an expected end."*

JEREMIAH 29:11

A t the age eighteen, I met the man I would marry. We had
known each other for about three weeks when we decided
to move in together. I knew it wasn't right, but I didn't
care. We lived together for three months before we got married. I
didn't know him well and he didn't know me. We jumped in with
all our baggage. Me with the weight of my past. Trying to figure
out how it was going to work. I loved him (still do) but I wasn't sure
if he really loved me. I didn't know until we were married the kind
if things he was into. I knew he did some things, but I didn't know
the extent of those things until we got married. I know finding all
that out made me question if we should be married. Was he going to
be able to change? I started to focus on his issues. If I could fix him
things would be good. I put all my energy in making sure he was

doing right. Pointing out the things he was doing wrong, so no one would see the mess I was. When I met my husband the only thing, I did up to that point was drink alcohol

and smoke cigarettes. After we met, I was introduced to drugs. I felt protected because he wouldn't let me do anything unless he was with me. I remember the feeling of being free from all worries or thoughts, no images leaving me anxious or scared. I was looking for something to help me with my pain and emptiness and I found it. I would take pills and drink which would make me sleep. I slept so much. But when I woke up it was back to feeling the same way. The images were still there. The pain and emptiness were still there. I don't blame my husband. I had a choice and I chose drugs and alcohol. I told him about the sexual abuse when we first met, part of me thought if he knew he would leave. There were times I wanted him to leave. Things were so messed up and I just kept making a bigger mess. There were times when I wished I didn't tell him. I was sure he thought I was disgusting. How could he love me? I was damaged. Undeserving of love. Even though we had our issues, there was always one thing I knew deep down. He loved me. Which is why I spent so much time trying to sabotage my marriage. I felt undeserving of his love, just like I felt undeserving of God's love.

When we were married 5 months, I found out I was pregnant. My husband was upset. He wasn't ready for a baby. Neither was I. He was still out partying, and I was questioning if we should be married. Adding a baby to our messed-up life didn't seem fair. How was I going to love a baby when I couldn't love myself? How was I going to take care of a baby when I couldn't take care of myself? My first thought was abortion. I was nineteen and I didn't have my life put together. I didn't want a baby. After some time, I thought about giving the baby up for adoption. That way the baby would have a chance at a good life. I wouldn't be able to provide the things the baby needed. I didn't tell anyone what I was going through. Everyone thought I was happy to be having a baby. I wasn't. As I watched my stomach grow, I felt love. I decided no matter what happened I would keep my baby. I knew it would be hard. But I couldn't give away my baby. I was going to figure out how to love my baby. A week after my husband and I celebrated our one-year wedding anniversary I gave birth to a healthy baby boy. I promised my son that I was going to do everything I could to protect him. I was going to be the best mom I could. I was going to learn to take care of me, so I could take care of him. But how was I going to take care of me when no one knew what I was dealing with.

When my son was almost two, I had another baby boy. I was putting my identity in being their mom. I was still drinking. Mixing prescription pills in with the drinking. I was miserable. I wasn't being the mom my boys needed.

In 2007 I had a two-year-old, almost three-year-old boy. Plus, an almost one year old boy. Things were hard for me. I found it hard to be a good mother to them. I was so caught up in my own mess that I wasn't taking care of them the way I should. I didn't really have any boundaries in place when it came to them. I allowed others to treat me and my boys any way they wanted. I never spoke up. I didn't know how to be a mom. My marriage wasn't good. I felt like everything was falling apart. I couldn't be there for my family. I was looking for ways to escape my pain. Fussing at my husband for doing wrong, all the while I was doing the same thing. One day I was on the computer, and I found some porn sites. I knew it wasn't me. I figured it was my husband. I thought he was different than any other man. When I saw that I couldn't believe it. He wasn't the man I thought he was. Seeing that made me feel disgusting with myself. I thought it was my fault he turned to that. I also thought he wanted me to look like those women and be like them. My view on sex was already distorted. This just added to it. I asked him about the sites, and he denied it was him. I felt like I couldn't trust him anymore. He lied to my face. I never thought he would be the one to hurt me. I packed my stuff along with my boys and we left. I used that as an excuse to run away. I could have stayed and talked it through with him. But I thought this was my chance to leave him before he could leave me. Which would be something I did a lot of in the years to come. Not talking about things. Just running away from my problems. We were separated for almost 4 months. During that time, I would spend almost every weekend getting drunk. Drinking numbed the pain. It made me forget everything I was going through. Not just the abuse I had endured but also with my marriage. Instead of dealing with my issues, I would push them all down. I figured if I ignored them, my problems would all go away. Running away from my problems would be something I continued to do for years. When we got back together, we moved to where my husband's dad lived. It was another way for me to run away from things. But what I tried to run away from was still with me. I was still suffering from depression. I still had nightmares. I still couldn't sleep. I lived in fear. I hid who I was. Pretending everything was fine. Everyone loved on me. Welcomed me into their lives. They didn't know what I was dealing with. Shame kept me from reaching out to people. Even though I am sure that my in-laws would help me get help I couldn't tell. I didn't want people to see the real me. I wanted people to think that I had it all together. That my life was perfect. If they knew the real me, they wouldn't love me anymore. They would be disgusted with me. I felt disgusted with myself. I was living a lie. It had become my normal. We lived there for almost 6 months before we moved back to where we were living. I was pregnant with our third son when we decided to move. When I had my third son, I was dealing with postpartum depression. My post-partum depression only made things worse for me. I didn't want to do anything. I didn't want to feed him or bathe him. A friend of mine told me I should get help. I was just going to get help for the postpartum depression. When he asked if I thought about hurting myself or anyone else, I lied. My doctor prescribed me some medicine for depression. I could have told him the truth and talked to someone about what I was going through. I just didn't know how or who to go to. Taking medicine was something I didn't want to do. I was only on the medication for a little over a month before I stopped taking it. I didn't think I needed the medicine. I was taking care of my baby. I was doing things that I needed to do, but I was just going through the motions. Pretending to be alright. I just wanted people to get off my back. When my third son was almost a year old, my husband got laid off work.

We moved to where my family was living. I thought being there was going to help me. I was pretending that I was fine. I was doing what everyone else wanted me to do. It was like I couldn't think for myself or do anything on my own. Moving to where my family was didn't help me. But it didn't I felt like I was being someone I wasn't. I was about five months pregnant when we decided to move back to where we were living before. Looking back, I can see that God was setting things in motion. He had to put me where He wanted me, even if it meant making others unhappy. After our fourth son was born things got worse. I was diagnosed with postpartum depression. I would spend most days in my room, in the dark, crying, while holding my baby. I had so much resentment towards him. He wasn't planed. He wasn't supposed to be here. I felt like he ruined my life. I didn't want anything to do with him. When my son was almost a year old, I started to experience some back pain. So, I called the doctor who delivered my son and he prescribed me some pain pills. At first, I was taking them as prescribed. I stopped taking my depression medicine. I didn't think I needed them. I started taking the pain killers even though I was no longer in pain. I would take them like I was supposed to, until one day when I was really depressed, I took more. That got me hooked. I told myself that it wasn't abusing them if it was prescribed. But I wasn't taking them the way I should've. I took them to ease my pain. To make me numb. I just wanted to stay numb.

I was so numb I didn't know how to love my family. I couldn't feel anything. When I did feel something, it was anger, fear, shame, and guilt. I didn't want my husband or my boys hugging me or touching me. I allowed my boys to talk to me any way they wanted to. Most of the time I didn't want them around me. I tried to explain to my husband that it physically hurt me when he touched me. It was like I was feeling the pain from the abuse every time he touched me. Being intimate with him was hard. I always felt disgusted. We didn't have any connection. I felt like there was one thing he wanted. There were times where I was afraid to tell him no. Although I would never tell him. I wanted to be intimate with him. I just couldn't. Sex always brought me back to the sexual abuse and nothing I did could change that. I was having a hard time loving them. I couldn't even love myself. I love my husband and boys but I just couldn't show it. I was angry all the time. I would always yell at them. I was hurting so I wanted them to hurt. I didn't know at the time that I was projecting what I was feeling on them.

The only thing I thought would make me feel better was suicide. I wasn't thinking about anyone but me. I wasn't thinking about the pain I would put my family through. I just wanted the images to go away. I wanted the pain to go away. I couldn't be in the moment. I was always living in my past. Reliving the abuse every day. Feeling like it was happening all over again. Every second of my day was filled with doubt, fear, anxiety, depression, shame, and anger. I didn't see how there was any hope for me.

I started getting into some very dark things. I was so angry with God. I thought God was the reason for all my pain. Even though I grew up in church, the way I felt about God made it easy for me to go down the dark path I went down. When I say I got into dark things I mean things like the Ouija board, dabbling in satanic things. I can look back and see that what I was doing was exactly what satan wanted me to do. He had me where he wanted me. I was trying to fill the void I felt. It didn't matter what I filled it with. It was never enough, and it kept me wanting more. It kept me seeking more worldly things. I was believing in things that I knew were wrong. That deep void I felt was so deep, I thought if I filled it with things that made me feel good for a time then I would eventually find something to fill it so I wouldn't have that void anymore. It wasn't getting filled because I wasn't filling it with Jesus. He is the only one that can fill that void we have in our lives. No amount of drugs, alcohol, men, money, or whatever it is you are turning to can fill that void. Only Jesus can.

Holding in this secret. Not getting the help I needed, kept me in bondage. It kept me chained to my past. I was searching for anything that could help me with the pain and emptiness I felt. I didn't have to look far. All I had to do was look up. Deep down I knew that. I knew what His Word said. But Satan had constantly filled my head with lies. I couldn't see the truth. Yes, I knew what the Word said. I just didn't believe it. Keeping all this in was not only taking a toll on me but on my marriage and my kids.

As my boys got older. I started to become cautious of who they were around. I didn't let them go off and do things. I wanted them by me all the time. When they weren't with me, I was constantly worrying. Thinking of all the bad things that could happen. I know as a parent you will worry. But I took it to the extreme. I would have panic attacks just thinking about something happening to them.

I was trying to protect them, but I was also hurting them. I kept them from having a normal fun childhood. I put so much on my oldest son. When I was in my addiction, he was the one taking care of his brothers. While I was in bed, he was cleaning and making sure his brothers were fed. He was playing the role as the parent. I can't explain the way that makes me feel. Knowing all the pressure that I placed on my son, at the time I didn't think anything about it. I didn't care. I was messed up. The only thing I cared about was making the pain go away. It didn't matter who I hurt. All because I didn't want to get help. I lived in fear that it would happen to me or them. I remember getting myself together right before my husband came home. I didn't want him to know that I spent most of the day in bed. I would be so angry when he came home, the rest of the night would be spent with arguing with him.

I was so filled with guilt. I felt like I was ruining their lives. I didn't think I deserved to be their mom. I was a mess. All I was doing was messing up their lives. They didn't deserve the way I treated them. I couldn't even get myself better for my kids. I just thought they would be better off without me. They needed a mom that wasn't a mess. They needed a mom that would be there for them. That would allow them to do things. Instead of a mom that was always angry. Pushing them away. Not letting them do things. I thought God made a mistake when He made me their mom.

Chapter

THREE

> *"Remember ye not the former things, neither consider the things of old. Behold, I will do a new thing; now it shall spring fourth; shall ye not know it? I will even make a way in the wilderness, and rivers in the desert."*
>
> ISAIAH 43:18-19

My father-in-law would call my husband every other Sunday. When they talked my father-in-law would ask if we were going to church. My father-in law was always encouraging my husband to find a church for us to go to. Looking back, I am thankful that my father-in-law kept asking my husband. He was planting a seed for my husband. Which in turn led his family to church. God had His hands on me even then. I just didn't want to see it. I was in such a dark place that I couldn't see the way God was working. It all started with a phone call every other Sunday. God was using my in-laws. He will use anyone and anything to get you where you need to be. I knew my husband wanted to go. I always said I didn't want to go to church. I didn't want anything to do with God. Including going to church. My husband was trying to do the right thing, he was trying to lead his family, yet I wouldn't let him lead us. I was fighting hard.

In 2013 A friend of my husband invited us to go to church. We went but I didn't like it. It wasn't the church I didn't like. The church was a good one. I was just making excuses. I was still in a very dark place. The way I saw things were wrong. I didn't know what to believe any more. We ended up going to a different church that I believe now was where God wanted us. When we first started going to church, I wanted people to think that I was this perfect woman with this perfect life and a perfect family. My boys had to act like they were perfect, well-mannered little boys. How they acted reflected back on me. I didn't want people to think that I couldn't take care of my family. We all had to look nice so people would think that I had it all together. I lied and told everyone I was saved. I didn't want them to see the place I was in. I didn't want them to know me. I was covering up who I really was. Hiding behind a mask. The mask I was wearing was of someone who lived a perfect life. If I showed people, the real me. If they knew things I went through. The things I have done and the way I was still suffering, they wouldn't want to be my friend. So, I kept the mask on and kept everyone at a distance. I was a fake. I was afraid to let people in. I had been hurt and I didn't have a lot of trust for people. Especially men. I couldn't go anywhere without thinking that every man I saw wanted to hurt me. It made being out in public very hard. I didn't want to leave my house. I didn't think there would ever be a way out of the dark place I was living. It was getting so bad that if someone invited me or my family to their house or any outing, I would agree but the day of I would say I was sick so I wouldn't have to go.

My addiction to the prescription pills had gotten so bad that I would make excuses for me to go to the hospital. I would lie and say I was hurting, or I was sick. Just to get medicine. It didn't matter what it was. If it was strong enough to knock me out, I would take it. All I wanted to do was sleep. I didn't care anymore. I was tired. Tired of replaying the same images over and over. I was just tired. There was a time when I had to stop abusing prescription pills. Not by choice. I couldn't make excuses anymore. We didn't have the money for me to be feeding my habit. At one time I did think about selling them so I could get more. Looking at it now I know it was God that stepped in. He was protecting me. He was fighting for me.

Since I didn't have the pills anymore, I needed something to feel the void. So, I went back to food. I would buy boxes of snack cakes and I would end up eating the whole box in one night. I had so much shame over that. I didn't let my husband or kids know what I was doing. I would eat so much until I felt sick. I even started to throw my food up. I would eat so much. I would then feel guilty, and I would throw up my food. My husband would tell me that I needed to go to the doctor because it wasn't normal. He didn't know that I was doing it to myself. I was making myself sick. I liked the feeling. I felt like I was in control and I feeling sick like that made me feel something. It made me feel like I was in control. Everything else was out of control but I could control what I ate and how much I ate. I didn't know that it was a sickness. I would look in the mirror and think I was fat and ugly. I thought I was disgusting. Damaged. I was waiting for my husband to realize that he made a mistake when he married me. I was waiting for him to leave. I was always angry. Pushing him away and placing the blame on him. Always making him feel like he was worthless. That is the way I felt. Like I was worthless.

One day I went to my pastor and told him that I was sexually abused when I was younger, I needed to tell someone. Things were getting bad. I didn't think there would be any harm in telling him.

He showed that he cared. He prayed with me. For the first time in a long time, I felt like someone really cared about what I went through. Even though I felt that way. I still left a lot of things out.

I didn't tell him that I was still suffering so much that suicide was the main thing on my mind every day. I didn't tell him that most days I didn't feel like getting up and every night I would ask God to not let me wake up. I knew if I told him all that I would end up in a mental hospital. I knew I wasn't stable but if I admitted that to anyone it would shatter my perfect image. He gave me a video to watch. The video helped me a little, I watched it with my husband as well. I'm not sure if it helped him understand what I was going through, watching the video made a lot of things clear to me. He also gave me a number to a counselor. I went to counseling for a while. Only touching the surface. I knew I needed help, but I thought if I would just touch the surface. Put a Band-Aid on, I would be able to find some healing. But that was the problem. I wasn't digging deep; I was just trying to cover up enough so I could get through the day. Then I stopped going. It wasn't working for me. I felt the same. If anything, it made me feel worse. I just pretended that it was working and that I was fine. in public I would smile. I looked happy. But on the inside, I just wanted to die. Suicide was always on my mind. I thought it was the only way out for me. I would tell my husband that I needed to be in a mental hospital. I think that was scary for him. I don't think he knew how to take it so he would just laugh it off. Not being mean. He just didn't know what to do. It was hard for me to do the day-to-day things like clean my house. Taking showers or making sure my kids were fed and bathed. It was getting harder and harder for me get up in the mornings. I just wanted to sleep. I didn't want to do anything else.

It was getting harder for me to be intimate with my husband. Sex was always something I thought was disgusting. How could it be anything else. Growing up as a child who was sexually abused messed my mind up when it came to a lot of things. Especially sex. At the time of my abuse, I was so young I didn't really understand. It wasn't until I got older that the reality of what I went through hit me. It made me feel dirty, shame, disgust, and guilt. There were days when I would take a shower to try to wash away the way I felt. But no matter how many times I showered it was still with me. I didn't want to be in my own skin. I wanted another life. That is where writing comes in. I would write stories just to be somewhere else. I loved reading books. For a short time, I wasn't dealing with my reality. I could get lost in a book. It still didn't take away the pain I felt. It didn't take away my depression or thoughts of suicide.

My depression was getting worse. I was having bad anxiety attacks. Not to mention the PTSD. I was living in fear. Scared to leave my house.

Scared to do anything. I didn't think there was any hope for me. My family and friends didn't know what I was going through. They didn't know the struggle I faced every day. The pain I felt. The memories that wouldn't go away. The images that kept me awake at night. Afraid to go to sleep.

The scripture says "Do not remember the past events" I couldn't. I lived in my past. I couldn't be in the present. I would read my bible. I wanted to so bad to believe the things I was reading. But I couldn't. How could God allow something good to come out of the bad that I went through.

I just didn't think it was possible.

Chapter

FOUR

For God so loved the world, that he gave his only begotten Son, that whosoever believeth in him should not perish, but have everlasting life.

JOHN 3:16

In 2015 I was involved with a women's Sunday school class at church. We did many Bible studies and I tried to dig deep into the Word, but it was hard. I knew I wasn't in the right mind or had the heart for it. I wasn't saved. Reading the Bible was something I did at times. It was something I did so I could check that box.

We started doing a Bible study on secrets. There was something about this study. Something about what it was talking about that made me pay more attention. I was keeping a secret that was eating me up inside. That was the first time I really felt God tugging at my heart. Looking back now, I think God used that study to help me be able to be open about my past. After a few weeks of doing the Bible study I decided to be open and tell them about a secret that I was keeping inside. I just left out the way I was feeling at that moment. I didn't want them to think I was weak. I felt alone. I didn't think they would understand.

When I told them, they loved on me and prayed over me. I thought they were pretending. I was a little overwhelmed. The way they loved on me; it was like I was feeling God's love. When I started to let my walls down, thinking it was safe to let these women in, satan would fill my head with his lies. I listened to his lies. I started to build my walls higher to make sure no one, not even God could get through. Satan was telling me that I should have never told anyone. Keeping it in was the best thing. Satan told me that I wouldn't be welcomed back to church. I was damaged.

No one wanted me, not even God. I believed every lie satan told me in April of 2015 I decided to tell my mom what I had gone through. I felt like I had let her down. It was so hard to tell my mom that I was molested and raped. I thought she was going to be mad at me. The conversation we had didn't go the way I thought it would go. The things my mom was telling me were things I didn't agree with. My mom told me that I was strong. I tried to tell her that I wasn't strong enough to handle this. She told me that God made me strong. I hated that. I didn't feel strong. After all the things that I did, I knew I wasn't strong. God made a mistake. That sent me over the edge. Satan started telling me that all I ever do is let people down. He told me it would just be better to end my life. Everyone would be better off without me. I was a disappointment. I would always be a disappointment. God couldn't save me. He didn't want to save me. How could God love a mess up like me? God would never be able to use what I went through for His good. I could never do anything right. I was worthless and disgusting. Satan told me to go ahead and kill myself. All my pain would be gone. I wouldn't have to worry about living in my past anymore or letting others down. It was the only way I could get away from my pain. It would be my only escape. If I didn't, I would live with this forever. Always going through the same thing every day. It would be a never-ending cycle.

I had a plan in place. I knew exactly how it was going to happen. I had the date set. I was done. I was giving up. I couldn't handle the pain anymore. The weight was weighing me down. I couldn't function. My life was a mess. This seemed like the only thing I could do. I remember on a Wednesday night we went to church. It was two days before I had planned to end my life. As I was walking out of church. My pastor was standing shaking hands. I don't know what came over me. It had to be God. I asked my pastor if I could talk to him. We went into a room, and I told him what I had planned. He talked to me and prayed over. me. My husband was with me, and he had to make sure I didn't do anything.

The next day I went to see a counselor. I told her what my plans were. She wrote a prescription that she wanted me to take. Told me about a doctor she wanted me to see. She made me call my husband and talk to him all the way home. I was surprised that they didn't take me to the hospital.

I went to the doctor. Got put on some medicine for my depression. I started to see the counselor again. I still only scratch the surface. I told her about my abuse. I told her what led me to planning my suicide. I didn't tell her that I thought about my abuse every day. I told her I was depressed but not because of what I went through. I was still hiding. I never got my medicine refilled. Once it was gone, I didn't say anything. The medicine wasn't helping. I just didn't want to tell anyone. I wanted people to think that I was better. I was scared to say too much. I was still dealing with depression. I really didn't see an end to my suffering.

I started to think that I had a handle on my life. I didn't need anyone or any medication. There was nothing so far that seemed to be helping me. I felt like I was a lost cause. There was no hope for me. God wasn't going to help me. Why would He? After all I blamed him for everything bad in my life. I hated God for what I went through. I even hated Him for not allowing me to follow through with my plans to kill myself. God was ruining my life. Why would I want to serve Him? Why would I want anything to do with Him? That was the way I felt.

The summer of 2015 my mother-in-law invited us to go to a place called Celebrate Recovery. Celebrate Recovery is a faith-based recovery program, it is a program to help with any hurt, hang-up, or habit. I heard about Celebrate Recovery years ago and even went once. I just thought it was for people who are drug addicts and alcoholics. It wasn't a place for me. I thought I had a handle on my life, but I was in denial. The only reason I went to Celebrate Recovery was to support my mother-in-law. I didn't need help from anyone. Besides I tried to let people help me. It just never worked out. Part of the reason it never worked out was because I didn't allow the people to fully help me. I didn't allow them to get close to me. I had people I could turn to, I just kept them at a distance. The only thing I didn't do was give God a try. At that time, I wasn't planning on it either. I didn't see that God was coming after me. He was fighting for me. He was setting things in motion. I remember walking in Celebrate Recovery and feeling so overwhelmed. Have you ever walked in a room full of people and felt so alone? That is how I felt. I felt alone for many years, but this was different. There were so many people. I felt like none of them knew what I was going through. I was the only one who was suffering.

We were going to Celebrate Recovery for almost a month when I decided to go to small group. Small group is where you meet with people who are going through the same thing you are. I went into the co-dependency group. They had a class for abuse and depression

I went to that group one time, I decided it wasn't for me. I was at a place where I was denying the abuse even happened. wasn't ready to go there. I didn't want these people to know what I had gone through.

One Thursday night I decided to talk about my past. I told the ladies what I went through. I told them everything. I felt so vulnerable. I wasn't sure what my next step was. Until one of the leaders told me about a 12-step class. 12 step classes are where you get with women and go through your life. There are four books that you work through. I was a little unsure, yet I signed up anyway.

A week before I started taking the 12-step class my church had a revival. I was thinking anything was going to be special. I told everyone I got saved in 2014. I was good. Which was a lie. The only reason I went down in 2014 was because I figured it was what others wanted me to do.

I remember it was a Tuesday night. It was the third night of revival. I felt something that I couldn't explain. As soon as the evangelist stepped on the stage I started shaking. I knew in that moment my life was going to change. As he talked, I felt like God was speaking right to me. I remember closing my eyes. I saw myself in complete darkness but when I looked ahead there was light. It was like Jesus was standing there with His arms opened wide for me. I could feel the fight for my life. It was so strong. I didn't think God cared about me. But here He was. Waiting for me to come to Him. God wasn't going to force Himself on me, He doesn't do that. It was my choice. Did I want to stay in darkness or move to the light. That night I gave my life to Christ! It was so weird because that was the only night the pastor asked for the ones who wanted to get saved to raise their hands and make eye contact with him or the other pastors that were standing up front. I knew that was meant for me. When I went up front, a very sweet woman took me to the back and prayed with me. I remember crying so much and saying that I just wanted the pain to stop.

I could end my book here and say that all has been great since then. But that would be a lie. Things weren't great. I still suffered. I still dealt with the images. I still lived in fear. I still tried to find worldly things to help me ease my pain. I turned to things besides God. I still blamed God for the things I went through.

It took almost a year to finish my 12-step class. I didn't put all the work I should have put into it. I didn't do things the way I should have. I was lying to everyone. I only worked through small things. I never dealt with the big things, like the abuse. I said I did but I was just trying to get it done. I didn't want to work the steps. Did I get something out of it? Yes. But I didn't get what I thought I should get out of it, so I had my doubts. I told everyone that I forgave those who abused me. When I really didn't. I still had so much hate in my heart for my abuser. I didn't want to forgive them. If I forgave them, it meant that what they did was ok. I had a hard time coming to grips with that. Even though being at Celebrate Recovery I heard testimonies after testimonies of how God had changed people. I learned I wasn't the only one who had been sexually abused, yet I still felt alone. I still felt like no one understood especially God. I was still mad at God. He was removing things from my life. Things that I held onto things that I placed my identity in. My marriage was falling apart. My kids were out of control. I was going back and forth with taking my kids out of school to homeschool them, to putting them back in school because I couldn't handle it. One of the reasons I tried to homeschool was to prove to my mom that I could homeschool my boys. Whenever I would put them back in school, I felt like I failed them. I had a lot of doubts. There wasn't a lot of structure in our home. I just wanted to run away. I never told anyone, but I was still contemplating suicide. I just wanted to end my suffering. I started to have some health problems. I got hooked on prescription pills again. I would go to different hospitals to get my pain pills and other pills. I would take them so I could sleep. I was a mess. I didn't know how to stop. I didn't know if I could stop. How was I going to be able to come back from this? I told no one. I felt ashamed. I wasn't turning to God; He was always my last resort. In 2016 I told my husband that we should separate. I was pushing him away. Trying to get him to leave. I figured that I would be the one to leave. That way he couldn't hurt me when he realized he made a mistake when we got married. I was keeping him at a distance. I just knew that he was going to leave me. I thought I was protecting myself from being hurt. I had all these walls put up. No one was going to break them down. I didn't want anyone to get close to me anymore. I was always waiting for the other shoe to drop. When we separated, my husband never did move out. I slept on the couch, he slept in the bedroom. While we were going through this, I made things bigger than what they really were. I told a lot of lies about my husband to make him look bad. Only a few people knew we were separated. After about two months, we decided to try to work things out. Well not really him but me.

FIVE

> *"But now thus saith the LORD that created thee, O Jacob, and he that formed thee, O Israel, Fear not: for I have redeemed thee, I have called thee by thy name; thou art mine."*
>
> ISAIAH 43:1

I tried to get in the Bible and study the Word. I even had an idea to start a women's bible study group at my church. I was throwing myself in everything I could. Thinking that would help me heal. After all I was doing everything for Jesus. But I wasn't. That is a lie I told everyone. I was trying to stay busy. That just meant at night I wouldn't be able to sleep, and my anger grew. The hate grew. I cried out to God I don't know how many times. Begging Him to end my suffering. To end my life.

I didn't want to live if I had to live with this. I read about Paul in the Bible, having a thorn in his flesh. It never mentioned what the thorn was. I told God that if going through the abuse over and over was going to be the torn in my flesh, then He could just take me home to heaven. I didn't want to suffer. I didn't want to spend my days living out my abuse. It was too much for me to bear. I say that knowing that Jesus suffered for me. He suffered more. Yet I couldn't suffer a little.

Being a part of Celebrate Recovery was something that I loved, even though I felt like I didn't fit in there. I was always hiding how deep my pain was. Yes, I talked about what I went through, but I could never bring myself to be completely honest with the people there. At Celebrate Recovery we are told we can take off our mask. Our mask being something we hide behind. Let everyone think we are something we are not. Taking our mask off is being vulnerable. Letting others in. It was something I found hard to do. I had friends there that I talked to. I just didn't let them know how bad I was suffering. Celebrate Recovery is a safe place. Did I feel safe there? Not all the time, no. There were a lot of men, and I would get bad anxiety when I saw them. I was afraid they would do something to me. I thought that as a Christian, as someone who went through the 12-step class, someone who was a leader, that I should have it all together. I should have everything figured out. But I didn't. Did taking the 12-step class help me any? Yes, it did. There were things that I needed to let go of. I was finding healing and being restored in some areas of my life. Just not the ones I wanted healing from. I was getting mad at God. Here I was doing everything for Him. The only problem was I wasn't giving Him everything. How was He going to help me heal and move out of my past if I wasn't willing to give Him everything? I was holding back. Part of me feared what God would do with my broken pieces. Thinking that He would tell me I was a lost cause, and nothing would help me.

Part of me feared feeling something other than pain, other than the hate I had carried most of my life. I was scared. I wasn't trusting God. I struggled every day to let go of things. I wanted to be in control. I didn't want to leave my life in God's hands. I didn't want to let go of what I what I knew. I was holding on for dear life. Picking the parts of my life that I wanted God to control. Even then taking things back because He wasn't working as fast or in the way I wanted Him to. I would make a mess of everything. My family was falling apart. I told everyone I was fine. I walked around like I had it all together. Part of the reason why I didn't speak up about the things I was going through, is because I thought they were tired of hearing me talk about it. Even though they never said anything or acted in that way. It was all in my mind. A lie satan wanted me to believe. I kept the ladies at a distance. I was scared to get close to them.

I became a leader at Celebrate Recovery. I was leading 12 step classes, helping lead small groups. Helping other women. Yet I felt fake. I didn't believe a lot of the things I was saying. I wasn't sure if this was the place God wanted me. How could I help others when I couldn't even help myself?

We started going to a place called One-way on Friday nights. Which is a place like Celebrate Recovery. I got into a small group with some amazing women. I shared my struggles. There was still a lot of emotions when I talked about my abuse. Every time I talked about it, I felt like it was happening all over again. I would get angry. I wanted to be at a place where I was fine, where it didn't hurt every time, I talked about the abuse. To be ok with what I went through. But I just couldn't. I told everyone that God was going to use this for good, yet I didn't believe it. He hasn't used anything I went through for good. I had ladies tell me that I helped them. It was hard believing that. For the first few years of my Christian life, I filled everyday with church. Thinking if I was in church enough, I would be able to find healing. To find what I had spent years searching for. But I was just going through the motions. I often thought about my mom telling me I was called to be in ministry. To be a preacher. I didn't know how God could use me or why He would want to use me. I often walked around thinking about suicide. I knew if I said something I would be put in the mental hospital. I didn't want that. I wanted to stay in control of my life. Even though my life was a mess.

Chapter

SIX

"Before I formed thee in the in the belly I knew thee; and before thou camest fourth out of the womb I sanctified thee, and I ordained thee a prophet unto the nations."

JEREMIAH 1:5

I often thought about the conversation I had with my mom when I told her about my abuse. The words would replay over and over in my mind. It didn't matter what I said to her, it was like she wasn't hearing me. She just kept saying I was strong. I didn't feel strong at all. I hated God! I couldn't understand why He would allow this to happen to me. If this was His plan, why didn't He just end my life before I was born. That way I wouldn't be suffering. If He knew it was going to happen, why didn't He stop it? Why did He put me in situations for the abuse to happen? I didn't understand. That is what satan wanted me to believe. He wanted me to believe that God never protected me, that He didn't care about me, that He never cared about me. Satan wanted me to think that there was nothing more God could do for me. That He had left me. That's what I felt like. I felt like God left me. I blamed Him for causing me so much pain. He could have stopped the abuse. The truth I learned is that we all have free will. Yes, God knew what I was going to go through, but it wasn't His choice. We live in a fallen world. Sin is what the cause is. Not God. This isn't how He created the world. Everyone has a choice to make. Some choices go against the plans God has. But God can use anything for His glory. That is something I learned from Celebrate Recovery. Did I believe it all the time? Nope. But I'm human.

The anger I had was keeping me from living my best life. I didn't know who I was. I knew that living this way wasn't healthy. People knew about my past. They just didn't know how much I was still struggling and the thoughts that went inside my head. I never told anyone. I was suffering in silence. I wanted to tell people what I was going through. On the inside I was screaming. Does anyone care? Do they see the hurt? Do they know how much I don't want to live? Will, someone please help me! That was always going through my mind. Then satan would say. No one cares. Why would they. Look at you. You are disgusting. You are worthless. No one loves you. Everyone is just pretending. God doesn't even love you. I was battling everyday with these thoughts. It got to the point where I wasn't sleeping at night. I would stay up. Eating everything I could find. I would go to bed at six in the morning. Some nights I wouldn't sleep at all. I wanted these thoughts to go away.

I started to push my husband and kids away. In 2018 I was done. I didn't want to be around anyone. I told my husband I wanted a divorce.

I wasn't wanting to run from my husband. I just wanted to run from the pain and my thoughts. I shouldn't have reached out to someone. By the time I made up my mind to leave my husband it was too late. I wasn't going to listen to anyone. I was telling people it was what God wanted me to do. Which I knew wasn't true. Let them focus on my marriage so maybe they wouldn't see the struggle I was facing. These people were my friends. I called them family, yet I couldn't bring myself to be honest with them. I would lay down at night and beg God to end my life. It had to be better than what I was facing.

Keeping that in was eating me up. Deep down I knew what the problem was. I just didn't want to admit my problem and get help. I just tried covering it up. I was blaming my husband, kids, God even my church. I was blaming everything on everyone and not taking the blame for myself. My sweet friends would come to me and tell me that they saw me going down a dark road. I didn't listen to them. I brushed them off. I didn't want them to know what I was really going through. They wouldn't understand. I felt like I should be past all this and if people knew what the real problem was, they would look down on me. Think I wasn't good enough to be a leader.

I remember one Thursday night I was brought to a room with a pastor from our church and his wife. They wanted to talk to me about leaving my husband. I remember being so angry at them. Inside I was screaming. I'm hurting! I don't want to live anymore! I don't know how to get help! I had a chance to say something. They wanted to help me. They cared about me. I just couldn't let them. I felt attacked. I know now it was a defense mechanism. I was trying to protect myself. But I was really hurting myself more. I was turning away from everything and everyone. I even stopped going to the church I was going to. I went somewhere else. I was trying to run from God. But I couldn't. He was speaking to me through others. I was being stubborn.

I remember one night hearing my son pray that his parents would get back together and not get a divorce. That broke my heart. A friend of mine pointed out that not only was I leaving my husband I was also leaving my boys. I had stopped being there for them. How could I tell anyone that loving them was hard? I was an emotional wreck. Who would understand what I was going through? Not only was it hard loving my family, but it was too hard love myself. Hard to believe that God loved me, or anyone for that matter. The best thing to do was to leave everyone. Push everyone aside. The only thing I could think of was suicide.I am so blessed that God placed me and my family in a place where there were people who loved me. They prayed for me. Even though they didn't know what I was going through they still prayed. These people were fighting for my marriage. They were fighting for me. They would have done anything to help me if I just spoke up. I was overwhelmed by the support that was being shown. I never experienced anything like that in my life. It was new.

I was walking in the grocery store when God told me it was time to go back to my husband. When I told my husband, I wanted a divorce I also told him that I didn't love him anymore. I hurt him so much. I went home that night and we talked. I told my husband that I did love him. The only thing I left out was the main reason I wanted to leave. I didn't tell him I was still struggling with my past. I knew he didn't understand. He didn't go through what I went through so he wouldn't know how I was feeling. I couldn't tell him or my boys that I was hurting so much I just wanted to die. I put on a smile and acted like I had it all together. Which I didn't. I had nothing figured out. I was still angry. Still had hate in my heart. I took my anger out on my kids and husband. They didn't deserve the way I was treating them. In 2019 God laid it on my heart to homeschool my boys. I didn't know why He did. I was a mess. I was sure I was going to mess them up. But I followed God's leading. He provided everything we needed. I still don't know why God wanted me to start homeschooling my kids. But I am doing it.

Two years later in 2020 I felt like I was strong enough to be able to move past my past. I told myself that I was fine. Things were good. It was all a lie. I was going through the motions. The things I posted on social media was fake. I was pretending things were good. My anxiety was bad. I didn't want to go anywhere.

Then we got hit with a pandemic. We were on locked down. Couldn't leave the house. Had to wear a mask. I couldn't wear the mask for very long. I would have panic attacks and had to leave the store. My husband had to do most of the shopping for us. I know that was hard on him. I tried to explain the reason why I couldn't leave. I think he understood a little. I felt alone. Who was I going to turn to? That is when things got bad for me. I would have panic attacks in the stores. Wearing the mask made me feel like I was being suffocating. It brought me back to my abuse. I spent almost every weekend in my closet crying. I told my family daily that I wanted to leave. I cried out to God to just end my life. I didn't want to do anything. I stopped reaching out to my people. I then got mad when no one reached out to me. They didn't know what I was going through. I didn't want anything to do with God. I felt like He let me down. That He didn't take this from me. I gave up on Celebrate Recovery. I was running away. I didn't need God, Celebrate Recovery, church, or the people God placed in my life. I was miserable. My family was miserable. My husband was always afraid he would come home, and I would be gone. He tried to help me, but he couldn't. I couldn't leave the house without one of my boys with me. I was terrified to leave my house. All I could see was the rape and molestation happening all over again. I was scared to be alone, scared to leave my house. I was hitting rock bottom. Once again suicide became something that consumed my everyday life.

SEVEN

"Fear thou not; for I am with thee: be not dismayed; for I am thy God: I will strengthen thee; yea, I will help thee; yea I uphold thee with the right hand of my righteousness."

ISAIAH 41:10

About the summertime of 2020 I thought we should try to have family day. No video games, no phones, no T.V, just us being together, but all that happen was me getting mad and yelling at everyone. I would end up in my closet begging for God to take my life. Only God knew this. I didn't tell anyone what I was going through. I didn't think they would understand. How could I tell my husband that I was so angry at what was done to me years ago? He wouldn't understand. He couldn't because he didn't experience it. I felt like if I told him, he would just tell me to get over it. Like he had in the past. It really did keep me from reaching out to others. It also kept me from talking to him about it. I knew he didn't mean it the way it sounded. But at the time it fueled my anger. How could I tell my boys that I lived in fear of being sexually abused again?

The abuse started when I was a young girl. But it happened as I got older. When I talk about sexual abuse, I don't just mean inappropriate touching. I am talking about being molested and raped. It took me a long time to say the word rape. In my mind rape was a woman yelling telling her abuser to stop and her getting beaten. Rape to me wasn't saying no then laying there and letting it happen. Maybe that is why I thought it was my fault. I thought I let it happen. I didn't do anything to stop it. If only I would have fought harder. If only I tried to run away. Maybe I wouldn't be suffering like this. That is what I constantly thought about. It doesn't matter. If you say no and they continue it is rape. It doesn't matter how old you are. It isn't right. It isn't your fault. It took me awhile to come to that realization. When I was first raped, I was a little girl. The last time I was eighteen. So, you see it wasn't a onetime thing. It was something that happened to me many times. Leaving me dead inside. Leaving me searching for things to fill the void inside. Even after I got saved, I was still looking for worldly things to fill the big void I had in my life. I wasn't turning to God. He is the only one that can fill the void in our lives. I just didn't know at the time. God was who I needed to be running to instead I was running from Him. I was pushing everyone away. The trauma I experienced took a toll on my everyday life. It affects everyone differently. Even though I did go down a dark road, I know it could have been a lot worse. Sexual abuse is something that doesn't always have physical scars. The scars we carry can be emotional and mental. Like me, I suffer from a lot of mental illness due to my trauma. Sexual abuse can keep us locked in our own minds; it can keep us from forming healthy relationships. I know it did me. Since sexual abuse is something that isn't talked about a lot, it can keep you from seeking help. A lot of the times, sexual abuse happens by people we trust. Like family members. That alone can make it difficult to get help. Turning to the world isn't going to help you, real hope, real help comes from Jesus!

I felt like God had left me. Like He left me alone in my suffering. That He didn't care about me anymore. I thought no one cared about me anymore. I was done with life. I thought about taking prescription pills again, we had some. It was in my reach. I wasn't going to take them to make the pain go away for a time. I was going to take them to make the pain stop for good. I was tired of feeling the same way every day. I was tired of being depressed. Tired of living in fear. Tired of the images that plagued my mind daily. I was someone I didn't even know. I was sure my husband and kids wanted me gone. They would be better without me. I was never going to be ok.

When church opened back up, I made every excuse not to go back. I didn't want to go and hear about a God who loves me. I didn't feel that He loved me. I even stopped going to Celebrate Recovery and said I wanted to step down as a leader. I didn't think it was for me anymore. I had been going there for five years and I was still dealing with the same old things. Nothing was going to change. To me it was just another thing that didn't help me. The reason why it wasn't helping me was because I was giving God everything. I was holding on to so much stuff. Hate consumed me. It was the only thing I felt, and I wasn't ready to let that go.

In October of 2020 we started going back to Celebrate Recovery. I really didn't want to, but my kids really wanted to go. I heard about another 12-step class that had just started. I ended up joining. Wasn't sure why. I didn't think it would help me. My husband was telling me I needed to go talk to someone. It was hard for him to see me the way I was. He kept trying to get me to get help. I didn't want the help. I knew I would be put on medication and if I was put on medication that meant I wasn't trusting God to help me heal. I was turning to man not God. My husband told me about taking medicine for a headache. He said it was the same thing. Or someone taking medicine for high blood pressure. It didn't mean I didn't trust God. The 12-step class that God placed me in was filled with amazing women, and for the first time since I started Celebrate Recovery, I felt like there was hope. I was surrounded by a group of women who loved me. They never judged me. They were there for me. They celebrated with me, prayed for me, and encouraged me. I knew that God placed these women in my life for a purpose.

In January of 2021 I decided to call a place called the Phoenix center. It is a behavioral health place. I made an appointment and a few days later a woman called to give me an assessment. I scored very high on everything! When she told me that I scored the highest on the PTSD assessment, I couldn't believe it! I talked about having PTSD but I never thought I had it. I mean PTSD was for people who had been in the war, right? The woman who gave me the assessment told me she could tell by the sound of my voice that I struggled with PTSD. In that moment, I started to understand why I was the way I was. I was diagnosed with PTSD, bipolar, social anxiety, and anxiety. For the first time I was seeing a light at the end! I was so ready to find healing. When she asked if I had any suicidal thoughts, I lied and I told them I wasn't having any suicidal thoughts. I knew where I would end up, I didn't want to go there. I met with a doctor who prescribed me some medicine. Along with taking the medication I met with a therapist. My therapist gave me tools to use to help me be able to handle my PTSD and anxiety. Going to church and Celebrate Recovery, seeing the therapist, and taking the medicine was helping me to be able to come out of my depression. I was learning things that I could do to be able to change my thinking. Meditations that

I could use. I had to train my mind to not think on the things of the past. The Bible says," *and be not conformed to this world: but be ye transformed by the renewing of your mind, that ye may prove what is that good, and acceptable, and perfect will of God.*" (Romans 12:2) I had to renew my mind. I had to think on things that are pure and good. God's word says in Philippians 4:8 "*Finally, brethren, whatsoever things are true, whatsoever things are honest, whatsoever things are just, whatsoever things are pure, whatsoever things are lovely, whatsoever things are of good report; if there be any virtue, and if there be any praise, think on these things.*"

I had to think on things that were true. The truth was I was safe. My abusers couldn't hurt me anymore. Thinking on my past was only hurting me. Holding on to resentment and anger was only hurting me. It was also keeping me from a deep relationship with Christ. The more I thought on things that were good like the Bible says the empty feeling I had got smaller and smaller. God was filling me up with His love, His grace, His mercy, and His Word. My husband and my boys were not used to seeing me in a good mood. My husband wasn't used to me letting him touch me and hold me at night. My kids weren't used to me not yelling. I was becoming someone new. 2 Corinthians 5:17 says "*Therefore if any man be in Christ, he is new creature old things are passed away; behold, all things are become new.*"

I rededicated my life to Christ. I stopped blaming Him for the actions of others. He was making me someone new. I was able to be in the present and not live in my past. I was getting more out in my 12-step class then I did in any other. In January God told me this was going to be my year for breakthrough. He really meant it. Things have not been the same for me. My marriage isn't the same. I never thought I would be able to feel as close to my husband as I do now. We are going on almost eighteen years of marriage. Right now, though it feels like we just got married. My love for him has grown so much. We have gone through a lot of hard times. My husband could have easily left. I was a mess. I wouldn't have blamed him for leaving. When I got help, I thanked my husband for sticking with me. He said, "You stood by me in my dark times, now it is my time to stand by you." Marriage is hard, especially if you don't have God in the center. But when you let God be the most important relationship it makes every other relationship fall into place. My marriage is being restored. I am working on rebuilding the relationship with my boys, especially my oldest. I know there is still some hurt and resentment on his side. I'm giving it to God. I know that He will work things out in His perfect time. Our home is a place of peace (as much peace as possible with four boys). I never thought I would be the person I am today. But God! Do I still have bad days? Yes. Do I let those bad days make me angry? Nope. Is it easy? Absolutely not. How do I manage when I have those days or those moments? Well, I first go to God. Read His Word. Listen to worship music. Remember that I am in a safe place. Also reaching out to the people that God has placed in my life. I don't run from my feelings. I don't eat my feelings. I admit them and deal with them. Pushing them down isn't healthy and all it does is make me bitter. What I went through wasn't God's fault. He wasn't punishing me. But He is using it for His glory. Could He have stopped the abuse? Yes. Does it mean that he loves me any less because He didn't stop the abuse? No. He is using what I went through for His good. The actions of others are something I can't control. But I can control how I handle it. I chose to let God use it the way He sees fit. When I said I was called into ministry, I believe it now. I think God is going to use what I went through to help others. I pray it does.

I had to come to a point where I had to forgive my abusers. Not forgiving them was keeping me at a distance with God. We are to forgive others just like Christ forgave us. That was a very hard thing to do. I didn't want to forgive. That is the one thing that I was still holding onto. That is the one thing I wasn't ready to give to God.   One Thursday night at Celebrate Recovery the pastor was preaching, and he looks out to where I was sitting and says "Let it go. Forgive that person." I knew that was God speaking to me. I forgave the ones who abused me. I forgave the one who took my childhood away. I forgave them. The freedom I found when I released that was something I can't explain. I have a deeper relationship with Christ. I am once again a leader at Celebrate Recovery. I am involved in my church. I homeschool my four boys. I share with everyone what I went through. Not for me to boast but so people can see what God can do if you just give Him a try, I promise you won't regret it! He took someone that was broken and is restoring her. He is taking my mess and turning it into a message. Beauty from ashes. The lies that satan told me I no longer believe. I am strong because of who lives in me. God is the only one who could heal a broken girl. He is the one who keeps me going. Nehemiah 8:10 says *"the joy of the LORD is your strength."* I have a joy that no one can take away. A peace that only comes from the LORD. John 14:27 says *"Peace I leave with you, my peace I give unto you: not as the world giveth, give I unto you. Let not your heart be troubled, neither let it be afraid."*

I was looking to the world to bring me peace. To make me happy. But the world can't. Not the way Jesus can. Did God completely heal me of my past? No. Am I mad at God for that? Not at all. Why? Because He has placed me in the right places to continue to find healing and be restored. I wanted a quick fix. When I didn't get what I wanted I got mad. Like a child throwing a fit. We live in a world where we have to have everything now. But God isn't like that. He has His own timing.

Isaiah 55:8-9 says *"For my thoughts are not your thoughts, neither are your ways my ways, saith the LORD. For as the heavens are higher than the earth, so are my ways higher than your ways and my thoughts than your thoughts"* He knows what is best. Things are still hard, but I serve a God who loves me. He has redeemed me. I am the daughter of the Most High. I am cherished by the maker of heaven and earth. He is for me so nothing shall be against me. He will never leave me nor forsake me. I am not defined by my past. My identity is found in God and Him alone. I am not my past; I am not my mistakes. I am not who the world says I am. I am who God says I am.

I am here to tell you that there is hope. You can find freedom from your past. You don't have to live in fear. You don't have to carry the weight of what was done to you. It isn't your fault. God is reaching out His hands to bring you into His comforting arms. Matthew 11:28-30 says *"Come unto me, all ye that labor and are heavy laden and I will give you rest. Take my yoke upon you and learn of me; for I am meek and lowly in heart: and ye shall find rest unto your souls. For my yoke is easy, and my burden is light."* It took me some time to see that I could trust Jesus. That He is for me. I had to come to a point where I was completely broken. The years before wasn't a waste. God was working on me. He was preparing me for what He had in store for me. I had to be at a place where I was willing. I wasn't willing before. He had the place and the people already picked out for me before I was even born. He has a plan for me and nothing I did or nothing that was done to me was going to stop His plans. What I went through was rough I lost a lot of things, but His Word says in Joel 2:25 *"And I will restore to you the years that the locust hath eaten, the cankerworm, and the caterpillar, and the palmerworm, my great army which I sent among you."* He really is restoring me. Not only me but my family as well. This road to healing hasn't been easy, but I wouldn't change it. I am thankful for what I went through. I am thankful for the lessons I learned and the wonderful people I have met along the way. God saved my life many times. He kept me here to fulfill His purpose and I believe that is for me to help others who have gone through what I went through. So many people don't talk about it. I was one of them. I find healing in sharing. It is still hard. I still struggle and I may always struggle. This could be the thorn in my flesh like Paul wrote about in 2 Corinthians 12:7-9 *"And lest I should be exalted above measure through the abundance of the revelations, there was given to me a thorn in the flesh, the messenger of satan to buffet me, lest I should be exalted above measure. For this thing I besought the LORD thrice, that it might depart from me. And he said unto me, My grace is sufficient for thee: for my strength is made perfect in weakness. Most gladly therefore will I rather glory in my infirmities, that the power of Christ may rest upon me."*

I know that God will continue to give me the strength I need to be able to get through each day. The days where I feel like I can't anymore. He will give me His strength. When I want to give up. He will be there. If I am willing to allow Him to continue to work in my life. I know there is nothing He can't do through me. This isn't my story. This is His story. Every day He is teaching me how to depend on Him. I may not be healed. It may not have gone the way that I wanted it to go but it happened the way He planned it. I did find healing, but most importantly I learned how to trust God and let Him be in control. I'm not the same person I was. I am becoming the person God has called me to be. I believe my calling is helping others. I am proof that you can move past the hurt. That you don't have to live your life the same every day. I realize that what I went through isn't something that defines me. I can let it define me and I have. Which caused me a lot of pain. Not only did I hurt myself, but I hurt the people that are close to me. I know I can't live with the regrets. I have to keep moving forward. Looking back over the years. Seeing the damage, I caused my family helps keep me on the path that God has set in front of me. The bible says that Jesus leaves the 99 to find the one lost sheep. Well, I heard that sometimes the shepherd has to break the sheep's leg. That is what God had to do. He had to break my leg to keep me from running away again. When things get hard, I tend to run. God is showing me that it is alright to feel the things I feel. I can't deny my feelings. When I am having a hard day. I need to remember to reach out to others. Not keep it in. I will have hard days. But during those times is when I need to cling to Jesus more. Let Him carry me. I need to speak about what I am going through. Not hold it in. There is nothing wrong with seeking help or taking medication. You can move past the hurt, the pain, the shame, the guilt, even the anger. It may not happen in your time. But it will happen in His time. You may not find healing the way you thought you would, I know I didn't. I thought healing would be not feeling the pain, or remembering the times I was abused, it didn't happen like that. My healing Is learning how to not let those things get me angry. My healing is learning to lean on Jesus. My healing didn't happen overnight. It is taking time. I am ok with that. God is teaching me how to be still and trust Him and not run away from my feelings. When things are hard, I'm learning to reach out to Him, even when things are good, I'm learning to praise Him. There is hope and His name is Jesus! I pray that God's story will help others. I know what it is like to want to give up, to feel like there is no hope. Going through life with the identity of someone who was raped or molested was hard for me. As you read, my life was anything but perfect. Even after I gave my life to Christ, I still struggled. The pain was so deep, the hate consumed me. It took a lot to get me to my breaking point. When I hit rock bottom. The only thing I could do was look up. I tried everything but God. Doing this on my own wasn't helping. I was just sinking further and further into darkness. But God! That is when He rescued me. I had to get out of the way so God could rescue me. I have given Him control of my life. I still deal with PTSD, it isn't easy, but God always makes a way. Please if you are struggling, get help. Speak up. Don't keep it in. Let someone know, someone you trust. I am praying for you. I love you, but most importantly God loves you!

Printed in the United States
by Baker & Taylor Publisher Services